Devoted:

A Feminist Analysis of Disability Fetishism

by Philippa Willitts

Devoted: A Feminist Analysis of Disability Fetishism
Philippa Willitts
Copyright 2013 by Philippa Willitts

Acknowledgements

Thanks to Garine' and Nayiree Roubinian for editing this essay, and first publishing it in the Rain and Thunder feminist journal.

Thanks also to Claire Donnelly and Yngve Digernes for many conversations on the subject which helped me to extricate the politics of some of the issues involved.

Why I Wrote This Essay

I have been concerned for some time about the existence of disability fetishists, but until recently had no idea of the extent of some men's obsessions or the lengths to which they can go to fulfil their fantasies about disabled women. I wanted to look at this further, and found that although there were various articles written on the subject from a disability rights perspective, and from the fetishists' perspectives, there was very little written from a feminist perspective, especially by disabled feminists.

I particularly wanted to look at the links between the objectification of disabled women by fetishists and the objectification of women in mainstream society, and to look at the extra issues around what the attitudes of disability fetishists say about societal stereotypes of disabled women.

Devoted: A Feminist Analysis of Disability Fetishism

Disability Fetishism takes three main forms: Devotees, Pretenders and Wannabes. Devotees are sexually attracted to disabled people; pretenders frequently pretend to be disabled themselves by using mobility aids or tying up their leg when bent, to appear to be an amputee; and wannabes actively want to become disabled, and will sometimes seek an amputation of a healthy limb to fulfil this desire.

There are overlaps between the three, in particular with many devotees also being pretenders or wannabes but for the purposes of this piece, I am concentrating on the phenomenon of devotees. The vast majority of devotees are white, heterosexual males and most are attracted to women with amputated or missing limbs. Other devotees fetishise different aspects of disability such as crutches, wheelchairs, leg or back braces, casts, or other impairments such as para- or quadriplegia. There appear to be fetishists for virtually every type of impairment. Rather like Internet Rule 34 *(1)*, if it exists, there are men who fetishise it.

Men fetishising certain parts of women's bodies

is nothing new, but what I want to explore is whether part of that objectification is in fact doubly offensive and dangerous because it is eroticising what is in fact a perceived helplessness, based on a reductive stereotype of what disability means. This not only causes the damage that we know that sexual objectification does to women, but it adds a layer of disablism *(2)* to the discourse, with a perception that disabled women are inherently weak, passive or desperate.

Individual devotees usually have a specific obsession, and women not meeting their requirements are of no interest to them. In reading about this phenomenon I had to become familiar with many codes used to denote a devotee's preference, especially with regard to amputee women. DAK is double above knee amputation, DAE is double above elbow, SBK is single below knee, and there are more than a dozen such codes, all familiar to, and used by, devotees in online discussions. These reduce women from being a woman, to being an amputee, and finally to the particular characteristics of her impairment alone. If a man fetishises a woman with one leg amputated above the knee, then a woman with both arms missing below the elbow is of little interest. Whether it is her right or left side can even be important.

Dr Robert Pollack, a lecturer in psychiatry, explains that, "The thing that turns them on has nothing to do with the whole person; it has to do with the characteristics of amputation" *(3)*, and Richard Bruno, the Director of the Post-Polio Institute in New Jersey, that, "an actual relationship would cause the disabled individual to become a 'real person,' making projection of the DPW's [devotee, pretender, wannabe's] own needs difficult or even impossible" *(4)*.

There is a lot of concern not just about the attraction that devotees have to disabled women but also about the actions they can take to fulfil their desires to see, interact with, and touch disabled women. One particularly disturbing pattern is that of devotees making careers of their obsession, such as, "Mike, a devotee from California, [who] has overcome this scarcity [of amputee women] by getting involved in activities central to the lives of those who have lost their limbs. In addition to working as a ski instructor for amputee skiers, he also volunteered at a local amputee-support group and at the Paralympics. In doing so he has come in contact with at least 1,000 female amputees" *(5)*.

Devotees are also known to work as prosthetists, orthotists, personal care assistants *(6)*, nursing, medicine, therapy, social work, and as volunteers in amputee support groups and rehab settings *(7)*. The potential for abuse by fetishists working directly with disabled women in these positions of power, frequently with legitimised physical access to their bodies, is clear and it turns the places which should be safe spaces of support, such as disability groups, conferences, and medical appointments, into threatening and dangerous places.

Gracie Rossenberger is an amputee and former director of the Amputee Coalition of America. She explains, "I think even worse than having to deal with the general devotee population is knowing there are those in professional positions who use us to feed their fascination on a daily basis. Yes, I've heard the rationalization that much of where we are today in the area of prosthetics is due to prosthetists with the "fascination". Well I would personally rather be a little further behind in technology than to question and squirm every time a prosthetist touches me because I don't know if he is or isn't a devotee. **How safe can we feel standing there partially dressed, totally vulnerable and exposed wondering if there is a hidden camera taking our picture that will end up in next months "new attractions" on the internet.** There are so many women whose pictures have been taken without their awareness that are now being viewed and used for fantasies by this population and we have no way to stop this hideous invasion of our privacy" *(8)* (emphasis mine).

In public, as well, disabled women are not safe from devotees' attention. One researcher found that, "Devotees do demonstrate problematic behaviors, ranging from collecting names, addresses and phone numbers of disabled persons, to obsessive and intrusive phone calls, letters and e-mail to persons with disabilities, attending and sometimes organizing disability-related events, lurking in public places to watch, take covert pictures of, talk to and touch disabled persons, and even engaging in predatory stalking. For example, over 85% of Nattress' sample agreed with the statement, "If I see a female amputee at a shopping mall I will follow her," and over 57% agreed that, "If I see a female amputee in a store I will try to talk to her" *(9)*, while another talks of devotees "cruising emergency rooms for new amputees in their spare time" *(10)*.

Elements of BDSM fantasy also appear in disability fetishism, particularly in relation to the equipment and aids associated with disability. Abasiophilia is a psychosexual attraction to people with impaired mobility, especially those who use orthopaedic appliances such as leg-braces, spinal braces or wheelchairs *(11)*. One abasiophilic man explains, "Then there is the vulnerability and domination aspect. Bondage is a strong turn-on for a surprisingly large number of people although many would not like to admit this is the case. Common in the bondage "scene" are leather leg and body harnesses, straps and buckles, and the more complex and restrictive the more is the turn-on. The similarity of bondage gear to orthopaedic appliances is remarkable. Orthopaedic bracing has a medical purpose whereas bondage is about restrictiveness leading to sexual pleasure. It is no coincidence that what turns on those in the bondage community is mirrored by LDWs [legbrace devotee wannabe] with leg-braces" *(12)*.

Related to this, an eroticisation of dominance is also evident. A devotee himself admits that, "a more disturbing characteristic of a devotee/amputee relationship is one of dominance. The acrotomophile is sometimes attracted to the amputee due to an innate need to dominate. This false perception of the amputee often leads to conflict" *(13)*.

This appears to be at least partially related to the perception of disabled women as weak, as well as an 'easy' conquest: "A preference for a disabled or disfigured, and therefore less threatening, more attainable or more easily dominated, 'love object' is a commonly-heard explanation for attraction to disabled persons" *(14)*.

Disabled women are already at a disproportionately high risk of sexual and physical violence. It is thought that 83% of women who have been disabled since childhood have been sexually assaulted, 49% of whom will experience 10 or more abusive incidents, and only 3% of cases are ever reported. Goodman, Dutton and Harris found that, "Lifetime risk for violent victimization was so high for homeless women with severe mental illness (97%) as to amount to normative experiences for this population" *(15)*. In addition, there are types of abuse which are specific to disabled women, such as forced sterilisation or forced abortion *(16)*, and "ridicule related to a specific impairment or the withholding of medication or mobility aids" *(17)*. Abusers are frequently also disabled women's carers.

Abuse of disabled women can occur not only in the home or in public, but also in institutions, group homes or medical settings, where disabled women might be more likely to experience violence than women living in the community" *(18)*. Jennifer Nixon, a Women's Studies tutor, also points out that "women living within institutions or care homes are much more isolated and have fewer opportunities for both disclosure of abuse and participation in activist work on this issue". Women with mental health problems or learning disabilities are much less likely to believed if they do disclose abuse, as they can be classed by the police as 'unreliable witnesses'.

As lesbian feminist activist and author Sheila Jeffreys notes, "The fetishising of disability comes from the way in which, under male dominance, male sexuality is constructed to eroticise hierarchy and to objectify" *(19)*.

It is interesting to see exactly what disability devoteeism tells us about how disabled women are viewed by society, and by those who fetishise them. There is a strong theme in many of the writings about a perceived weakness inherent to disabled women, which is fetishised by a man with a desire to dominate. Along with this is a strong message that disabled people are to be pitied, as tragedy has befallen them. This 'Pity Model of Disability' is always damaging in disabled people's fights for equality. Then there is the 'Aren't They Brave?' theme. This relates, of course, to the discourse of charity and pity, but turns disabled women into saints in these men's eyes. And finally, there is the 'she should be grateful for whatever she can get, after all she is damaged goods' attitude. Many women who do not fit the conventional beauty standard face this expectation.

One devotee says, "I personally think that some of the "wannabe" attraction is to the idea/role of infancy - ultimately helpless and ultimately powerful and pampered / taken care of, and at least some of the attraction to disability in others is to the role of being needed - a valued protector" *(20)*, while another states, "I have read of a young woman who stated that she was sick of being the subject of devotees' attentions. She was sick of hearing the word 'stump' and felt that it was only because she has a stump that men ask her for dates. I should like to ask this lady if she would be happier if young men avoided her because of her handicap. **I think that she should be pleased** and to choose somebody who likes everything about her" *(21)*, (emphasis mine).

In an interview with journalist Bob Guter, psychotherapist Alan Sable states, "Men have forced women to be, or to seem to be, less able, which led to the fetishizing of women's inability, or disability, if you will, the idea that women were attractive because they were the "weaker vessel" *(22)*.

Guter and Sable wrote about gay male devotees, but many of their observations about stereotypes of what disability means to devotees have some relevance for a discussion about heterosexual male devotees too, in terms of disability stereotypes and assumptions, and how these are eroticised.

Feminists understand that in a patriarchal society, men have a sense of entitlement over women's bodies. In this same society, many non-disabled people feel a sense of entitlement over disabled people's bodies. We are grabbed, pulled across the road whether we wanted to cross or not, our wheelchairs are pushed without our consent, and our views in our own healthcare are not always taken seriously, all in the guise of people "helping" us. Disabled people are also used to being stared at. It happens all the time.

With disabled women being both women and disabled (it may seem like overkill to state that explicitly, but many people do not see us as both, and do not acknowledge the intersection), societal sense of entitlement to our bodies is vast. In this context, the phenomenon of devoteeism makes even more sense, as an extension of how disabled people's bodies are 'other'ed.

Devotees, of course, justify their objectification and behaviours. They attempt to neutralise what they are doing by comparing it to other people who are attracted to certain body features, such as large breasts or red hair *(23)*, with no comprehension that any objectification of women, especially when based on a single, sexualised body part, is oppressive. This non-devotee male behaviour is hardly something to emulate, in terms of women's wellbeing or liberation.

Devotees will also even defend their stalking behaviours, as Kimberley Barreda explains.

"Some people argued angrily that they had a RIGHT to access us that way because of our rarity - our lack of interest in becoming their pin-up girls/guys meant nothing. One known harasser said "There aren't that many of you around, so I have the right to take your picture when I come across one of you"" *(24)*.

As I mentioned earlier, if a disorder exists, it can be fetished. I know at least two women who, while talking in eating disorder support chatrooms, have been propositioned by men who wanted to watch them vomit. The rationale of these men was, "Well, I like watching women vomit, and you like vomiting, so it's win-win". This kind of attitude by the men was a crude self-justification for exploiting vulnerable women who thought they were in a supportive place surrounded only by other women with eating disorders.

Another defence of disability fetishism is more complex. It states that objecting to devoteeism is the same as saying that it is wrong to ever be attracted to a disabled woman. The terms such as abasiophilia (an attraction to those with impaired mobility) and acrotomophilia (an attraction to amputees) actually pathologise the attraction as a mental disorder, a paraphilia *(25)*, and the effect of that pathologisation for a disabled woman can feel devastating.

About this Barreda, again, says that "according to a number of "learned" professionals and a small but vocal segment of the amputee community, if you think that [my being an amputee] adds to my attractiveness, you have a mental illness. [...] I am *so* horribly disgusting and deformed that anyone who is attracted to me *must* be sick" *(26)*.

There were many more accounts that I read of amputee women who were initially horrified when they discovered the existence of devotees, but then welcomed the attention as proof that their bodies could be seen as attractive and appealing.

Alison Kafer, Associate Professor of Feminist Studies at Southwestern University, explains that, "The cultural construction of women with disabilities as asexual, deviant, and unattractive affects the self-perception and self-presentation of disabled women, impelling them to disguise - and be ashamed of - their physical differences. Simply learning about the existence of men who found her attractive because of her amputation, not in spite of it, caused her to shift radically her understanding of her disability" *(27)*.

Society's insistence that disabled women's bodies be kept hidden - so that we don't offend - and chaste - because we are infantilised - is depressingly well expressed by Kafer here:

"Gayla Frank discusses the experiences of Dianne DeVries, a quadrilateral amputee, who frequently encountered criticism about her choice of dress during her stay in a rehabilitation facility. Frank explains that the medical team assigned to DeVries wanted her to wear cosmetic prosthetic legs, prosthetic arms, and long-sleeved, baggy clothing in order to reduce her disabled appearance. **Her refusal to wear these devices met with consternation from her doctors, who characterized her decision as a sign of "maladjustment," rather than independence**. Her preference for sleeveless dresses and tank tops was even more troublesome for the staff, who saw her appearance as "'somewhat unattractive and possibly disturbing.'" **Her medical team** encouraged more concealing clothing not in order to improve her physical functioning, but to make her appearance less shocking and disturbing for others. In the doctors' desire to make DeVries' disabilities invisible, they effectively made DeVries invisible; her opinions and desires about her own body, disability, and worth were ignored in their judgments of her actions as misguided, maladjusted, and unattractive" *(28)* (emphasis mine).

As long as disabled women, and in particular our bodies, are kept hidden away for the sake of the perceived oversensitivity of society, the less acceptance we can ever get as valid human beings. When Cerrie Burnell began her job as a presenter on British children's television, 'concerned parents' made a barrage of complaints to the BBC in fear that her missing lower right arm would scare their children *(29)*. Few appeared to think that it would, in fact, be an ideal opportunity to explain to their children that people come in all different shapes and sizes, and that there was nothing to be frightened of.

In such an atmosphere, how can disabled women feel free to stop hiding? Even if we lose our own self-consciousness, society imposes others' bigotry on us instead, as with all women. Megan Griffiths reports that "16.2% of disabled women had considered visiting a prostitute [...] because they find it difficult to meet people and hold down relationships, and desire human comfort and sexual relief" *(30)*. This is saddening, and a damning indictment of the effect that disablist attitudes have on disabled women. Considering the inaccessibility of many venues used for socialising and meeting people, and prejudice and discrimination against disabled people being so rife, in this context it is hardly surprising that many disabled women find themselves considering visiting a prostitute, or feeling glad of the positive attention of some devotees, when the message from everywhere else is that they are entirely unacceptable. Some disabled women participate actively in devotee culture, selling photos and videos of themselves. This is particularly understandable given that disability is a surprisingly expensive business *(31)*, and that women already find themselves in a worse economic situation than men.

Other women, however, interpreted devotees' attentions otherwise. The fact that devoteeism was a phenomenon, a fetish, or a niche interest reinforced to them that their bodies are so disgusting that "desiring disabled women may be seen as a 'condition' only 'afflicting' select members of the population". One amputee woman explains, "The defensive rhetoric of the websites confirmed my fears that the larger culture viewed women like me as unattractive and undesirable. Otherwise, I reasoned, why would such organizations even be necessary?" *(32)*.

These accounts are simultaneously shocking and not at all surprising. What can we, as feminists, do to ensure that disabled women stop feeling that their bodies are unacceptable, without requiring the male sexual gaze to affirm their attractiveness? Feminism has long been active on assuring women that our bodies are acceptable when fat, or hairy, or small-breasted, but we need to take on the issue of disabled bodies and what impaired bodies can look like. That women's bodies are always acceptable, regardless of the number of limbs, the number of scars, the number of wonky or broken or unusually shaped parts. We need to shout this loudly.

We also need to counter the idea that disability equals asexuality. It seems that some amputee women who take part in providing photographic and video materials to arouse devotees, do so, in part, to counter this idea. Kafer, talking about a woman who runs such a website, explains that "[Jama] Bennett herself suggests that ASCOTWorld serves as a site of empowerment for female amputees, resisting dominant cultural stereotypes about the asexuality of disabled women" and describes "her experiences within a culture in which the sexuality of the disabled body, particularly the disabled female body, is continually ignored, denied, or pathologized" (33). But how can we achieve the aim without contributing to the culture of the sale of images of women's bodies?

Disability is a state imposed by society which limits and oppresses people on the basis of their impairment and with these attitudes and behaviours, devotees are actually playing a part in disabling women. When part of our problem is that we are fetishised, objectified and sexualised by strangers, this adds to the other barriers we face in a disablist society. If it is true that most amputees that Gregson has come across would give anything to have their amputated limb back, this is arguably, in part, due to the behaviour of other people, societal prejudice and an inaccessible world. Given the suggestions of dominance being part of the attraction of disabled women to devotees, and the fetishisation of a perceived weakness, could this further oppression by means of intimidation even be part of the deliberate role of a disability fetishist?

Disabled women are used to mainstream society reducing them to their visible impairments alone. Devotees reduce women yet further, to eroticised specifics. And when I say reduced, I do not mean that the disability makes us lesser. I mean it in the same way that all porn reduces women to our breasts and vaginas. The inability to see disabled women as whole women is an everyday factor in a disablist society. The further reductionism from disability fetishists only serves to worsen this situation.

It is hard to disagree with R. Amy Elman's conclusion that "devotee publications contribute "to the second class safety and status of all women and girls, particularly those with disabilities"" *(34)*, and Nomy Lamm summarises the view of an amputee, quoting, "Either society denies our existence or fetishizes us like we're some hot taboo. Most of the world doesn't see us at all because of our disability. Getting attention solely because of it doesn't make it any better" *(35)*.

It is, of course, possible that individual women feel sexually empowered by the attention of devotees, just as there are non-disabled women who report feeling empowered by being viewed sexually. However, my overriding concern is the impact that men's fetishisation of women's body parts has on women as a whole, what message this conveys about women and how it affects our lives. Blaming individual women for this is misguided, as it can be fairly easily understood in the context of how women are socialised and how little power we can hold. This is then magnified in a culture where disabled women hold even less power, and have to strongly assert that we can be sexual beings at all.

So what can feminists do, in this culture of inaccessibility and disablist attitudes, to work against the objectification and victimisation of disabled women?

As well as empowering disabled women in terms of body image and self-esteem, it is clear that it is vital for feminists to work closely with female disability activists, to work to inform more disabled women about abusive relationships, and to look at the accessibility of services such as refuges and rape crisis centres. With the statistics we have seen here of not only the high occurrence of abuse of disabled women within relationships, but also the differing types of abuse which can affect disabled women and the difficulties in speaking out about them, disabled feminists must be enabled to be more actively involved in advising women's organisations about access and the barriers which stop disabled women from accessing services.

"Nor have disabled women's issues been fully taken up within the women's movement. Many participants from the disability sphere felt strongly that their interpretations of this set of needs were being marginalised or ignored by the refuge movement in the UK. Recent research on the needs of disabled women experiencing abuse has also found that 'a lack of awareness of disabled women's needs still pervades the domestic violence movement, despite recent attempts to improve'. Emily, a disability activist, most clearly articulated her frustration with what she perceived as a need for more attention to disability issues and disabled women within the domestic violence sphere: We're never invited on their platforms, you never see any disabled women on their platforms. They have nothing in accessible formats. And, also, we're not in their statistics" *(36)*.

The disabled people's movement must also take on the issues affecting disabled women, if they are to fight for the rights of all disabled people.

"Despite [...] similarities, the two movements [the feminist movement and the disability rights movement] have largely inhabited separate political spaces, working along similar trajectories for analogous goals but with little interaction on any specific issues. [...] The failure of the disabled people's movement to fully theorise the relationship between disability and gender has meant that the experiences of some disabled people, particularly disabled women, have not been fully acknowledged within the movement" *(37)*.

As feminists, we know that all women are vulnerable to male violence, and we know that this reality does not imply that women are inherently 'the weaker sex'. Similarly, admitting that disabled woman can be more at risk is not the same as following the disablist discourse that disabled women are helpless, needy and require pity. This is an important distinction to make. It is vital to avoid devaluing disabled people's existences when criticising devoteeism. It plays into the hands of those who patronise and oppress disabled people with pity and contributes to the view that disability is a terrible thing to be avoided at all costs.

Feminism needs to take up the issues of disabled women under patriarchy, not because disabled women need spokeswomen, but because disabled women ARE women. In order to tackle this, the barriers that disabled women face in accessing feminist activism need to be explored and dismantled. Disability fetishism must be added to the concerns that feminists hold about the objectification of women and girls. The stereotypes about disability which are perpetuated by devotees' fantasies need to be challenged.

The disability rights movement has a strong message: Nothing about us without us. Disabled women do not need non-disabled women to guess what we need and talk for us. We need an opportunity to speak, ourselves, and work together. Disablist attitudes within the feminist movement must be constantly challenged, as must misogynist attitudes in the disability community.

I refuse to choose between disability politics and feminist politics. I want the right politics, because disability and womanhood are not mutually exclusive. We don't have to betray one to honour the other.

About the Author

Philippa Willitts is a British freelance writer. She is a disabled feminist and her website can be found at www.philippawrites.com. She is @PhilippaWrites on Twitter

References

1. An internet meme which states that if something exists, then there is porn of it.
2. I use the term 'disablism' rather than ableism. Ableism is more commonly used in the U.S., but as a believer (broadly, though not uncritically) in the social model of disability, I know that people are disabled not by our bodies, but by the society we live in. The term 'ableism' suggests discrimination on the grounds of 'ability', which implies that it is an individual's ability that limits them, rather than the 'social, environmental and attitudinal barriers [which] dis-able people with impairments from being full participants in society' (Nixon). It is for this same reason that I prefer to describe myself as a 'disabled woman' rather than a 'woman with a disability'.
3. Gregson, Ian: "The Acrotomophile (or devotee), An Amputee's Perspective", http://www.amputee-online.com/amputee/acrotomophile.html, viewed February 2011.
4. Bruno, Richard L: "Devotees, pretenders and wannabes: Two cases of Factitious Disability Disorder" Journal of Sexuality and Disability, 1997
5. Gregson, Ian: "The Acrotomophile (or devotee), An Amputee's Perspective", http://www.amputee-online.com/amputee/acrotomophile.html, viewed February 2011.
6. Bruno, Richard L: "Devotees, pretenders and wannabes: Two cases of Factitious Disability

Disorder" Journal of Sexuality and Disability, 1997

7. Jeffries, G. Edward: "A Special Attraction To Amputees: Amputee Devotees", Overground Magazine, http://www.overground.be/features.php?page=THE&article=71&lan=en , viewed February 2011.

8. Gregson, Ian: "The Devotee Issue: Part II – The Opposing View", Amputee Online, viewed January 2011.

9. Bruno, Richard L: "Devotees, pretenders and wannabes: Two cases of Factitious Disability Disorder" Journal of Sexuality and Disability, 1997

10. Lamm, Nomy: "Fan Club", Nerve.com, 2000.

11. Anonymous: "Admirers, Devotees, Wannabes and Pretenders", Abasiophilia Information, http://sites.google.com/site/abasioinfo/Home/whatis, viewed February 2011.

12. *Ibid.*

13. Gregson, Ian: "The Acrotomophile (or devotee), An Amputee's Perspective", http://www.amputee-online.com/amputee/acrotomophile.html, viewed February 2011.

14. Bruno, Richard L: "Devotees, pretenders and wannabes: Two cases of Factitious Disability Disorder" Journal of Sexuality and Disability, 1997

15. Wisconsin Coalition Against Sexual Assault, "People with Disabilities and Sexual Assault", Information Leaflet, 2003.

16. Jeffreys, Sheila: "Disability and the Male Sex Right", Women's Studies International Forum, Vol. 31 Issue 5, 2008.

17. Nixon, Jennifer: "Exploring interaction between two distinct spheres of activism:

gender, disability and abuse", Women's Studies International Forum, Vol 32, Issue 2, March-April 2009.

18. *Ibid.*
19. Jeffreys, Sheila: "Disability and the Male Sex Right", Women's Studies International Forum, Vol. 31 Issue 5, 2008.
20. Anonymous: "The 1998 and 2005 Abasiophilia Surveys", Abasiophilia Information, http://sites.google.com/site/abasioinfo/Home/98survey , viewed February 2011.
21. Fritz: "A Prosthetist's Perspective", Overground Magazine, http://www.overground.be/features.php?page=THE&article=70&lan=en , viewed January 2011.
22. Guter, Bob and Sable, Alan: "How to find love with a fetishist", BENT, 2001, http://www.bentvoices.org/culturecrash/sable.htm
23. Gregson, Ian: "The Acrotomophile (or devotee), An Amputee's Perspective", http://www.amputee-online.com/amputee/acrotomophile.html, viewed February 2011.
24. Barreda, Kimberley: "Devotee Phenomenon", disthis.com, viewed January 2011.
25. "Paraphilia is a medical or behavioral science term for what is also referred to as: sexual deviation, sexual anomaly, sexual perversion or a disorder of sexual preference. It is the repeated, intense sexual arousal to unconventional (socially deviant) stimuli", from Stephen J. Hucker, "Paraphilias", http://www.forensicpsychiatry.ca/paraphilia/overview.htm
26. Barreda, Kimberley: "Devotee Phenomenon",

disthis.com, viewed January 2011.

27. Kafer, Alison: "Women: Amputated Desire, Resistant Desire: Female Amputees in the Devotee Community". Presented to Society for Disability Studies Conference, June 2000, Chicago

28. *Ibid.*

29. Saner, Emine: "TV Presenter Cerrie Burnell: I don't care if you are offended", The Guardian, February 2011.

30. Griffiths, Megan "Sex: Should we all be at it? A study into the struggles of disabled people's fight for sexual expression, and the implications of using prostitutes and surrogates to facilitate this sexual expression", 2006.

31. Joseph Rowntree Foundation: "Study exposes the extra costs of living that drive disabled people deeper into poverty", http://www.jrf.org.uk/media-centre/study-exposes-extra-costs-living-drive-disabled-people-deeper-poverty , October 2004.

32. Kafer, Alison: "Women: Amputated Desire, Resistant Desire: Female Amputees in the Devotee Community". Presented to Society for Disability Studies Conference, June 2000, Chicago

33. *Ibid.*

34. *Ibid.*

35. Lamm, Nomy: "Fan Club", Nerve.com, 2000.

36. Nixon, Jennifer: "Exploring interaction between two distinct spheres of activism: gender, disability and abuse", Women's Studies International Forum, Vol 32, Issue 2, March-April 2009.

37. *Ibid.*

Bibliography

- Aguilera, Raymond J.: "Disability and Delight: Staring Back at the Devotee Community", Bent Voices, http://www.bentvoices.org/culturecrash/aguilera_disability_delight.htm, viewed January 2011.
- Anonymous (1): "Admirers, Devotees, Wannabes and Pretenders", Abasiophilia Information, http://sites.google.com/site/abasioinfo/Home/whatis, viewed February 2011.
- Anonymous (2): "The 1998 and 2005 Abasiophilia Surveys", Abasiophilia Information, http://sites.google.com/site/abasioinfo/Home/98survey , viewed February 2011.
- Barreda, Kimberley: "Devotee Phenomenon", disthis.com, viewed January 2011.
- Bruno, Richard L: "Devotees, pretenders and wannabes: Two cases of Factitious Disability Disorder" Journal of Sexuality and Disability, 1997
- Child, Margaret: "What are disability paraphilias and who are devotees?", originally Overground Magazine, http://sites.google.com/site/abasioinfo/Home/who-are-devotees, viewed January 2011.
- Davis, Carol: "One-Legged Stardom", Overground Magazine, viewed February 2011.
- Fritz: "A Prosthetist's Perspective", Overground Magazine, http://www.overground.be/features.php?page=THE&article=70&lan=en , viewed January

2011.

- Gowland, Ronda: "Freak Fucker: Stereotypical Representations of Sexuality in British Disability
- Art", Disability Studies Quarterly, Vol 22, No 4, 2002.
- Gregson, Ian (1): "The Acrotomophile (or devotee), An Amputee's Perspective", http://www.amputee-online.com/amputee/acrotomophile.html, viewed February 2011.
- Gregson, Ian (2): "The Devotee Issue: Part II – The Opposing View", Amputee Online, viewed January 2011.
- Griffiths, Megan "Sex: Should we all be at it? A study into the struggles of disabled people's fight for sexual expression, and the implications of using prostitutes and surrogates to facilitate this sexual expression", 2006.
- Guter, Bob and Sable, Alan: "How to find love with a fetishist", BENT, 2001, http://www.bentvoices.org/culturecrash/sable.htm
- Stephen J. Hucker, "Paraphilias", http://www.forensicpsychiatry.ca/paraphilia/overview.htm, viewed March 2011.
- Jeffreys, Sheila: "Disability and the Male Sex Right", Women's Studies International Forum, Vol. 31 Issue 5, 2008.
- Jeffries, G. Edward: "A Special Attraction To Amputees: Amputee Devotees", Overground Magazine, http://www.overground.be/features.php?page=THE&article=71&lan=en , viewed February 2011.
- Johnston, Josephine: "Amputee Attraction:

Devotees and the Amputee World". InMotion, Volume 12, issue 3, 2002.

- Joseph Rowntree Foundation: "Study exposes the extra costs of living that drive disabled people deeper into poverty", http://www.jrf.org.uk/media-centre/study-exposes-extra-costs-living-drive-disabled-people-deeper-poverty , October 2004.

- Kafer, Alison: "Women: Amputated Desire, Resistant Desire: Female Amputees in the Devotee Community". Presented to Society for Disability Studies Conference, June 2000, Chicago

- Lamm, Nomy: "Fan Club", Nerve.com, 2000.

- Nixon, Jennifer: "Exploring interaction between two distinct spheres of activism: gender, disability and abuse", Women's Studies International Forum, Vol 32, Issue 2, March-April 2009.

- Paul: "Disability As A Symbol Of The Ultimate Other", Overground Magazine, http://www.overground.be/features.php?page=THE&article=75&lan=en, viewed February 2011.

- Saner, Emine: "TV Presenter Cerrie Burnell: I don't care if you are offended", The Guardian, February 2011.

- Tittle, Ken: "Wild Swans", Abasiophilia Information, http://sites.google.com/site/abasioinfo/Home/footbinding , viewed February 2011.

- Wisconsin Coalition Against Sexual Assault, "People with Disabilities and Sexual Assault", Information Leaflet, 2003.